Tonka® DRIVING FORCE

W9-BXY-614

Written by Craig Robert Carey
Illustrated by Isidre Mones & Ivan Vazquez

Power Lifting

SCHOLASTIC INC.

New York   Toronto   London   Auckland   Sydney
Mexico City   New Delhi   Hong Kong   Buenos Aires

HASBRO and its logo and TONKA are trademarks of Hasbro and are used with permission. © 2006 Hasbro. All Rights Reserved.

Published by Scholastic Inc.
SCHOLASTIC and associated logos are trademarks and/or registered trademarks of Scholastic Inc.

ISBN 0-439-83012-5

12 11 10 9 8 7 6 5 4 3 2 1   6 7 8 9 10/0

Printed in the U.S.A.
First printing, October 2006
Designed by Phil Falco

When a massive hole or trench needs to be made, call on the **excavator!** With one dip of its powerful bucket, it can remove huge boulders from the earth!

Dump trucks work with the excavator to haul away what the excavator digs up. It takes a lot of dump trucks to help, since the excavator works so fast!

These **cranes** tower high above the construction site! The crane's superstrong grapple is used to hoist beams and other building materials.

In places where trucks can't reach, the **heavy-lift helicopter** gets to work!

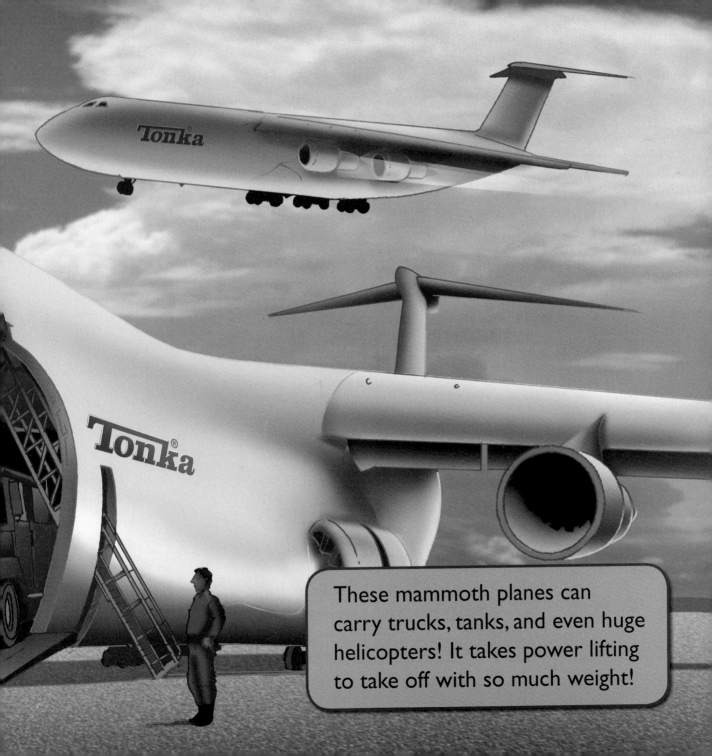

These mammoth planes can carry trucks, tanks, and even huge helicopters! It takes power lifting to take off with so much weight!

When a vehicle needs extra muscle and a boost of height, the **aerial** does the job! Aerials mount onto trucks to make tall jobs a snap!

An aerial can raise an entire crew of workers and hundreds of pounds of gear more than 300 feet into the air!

It might not be the biggest vehicle around, but the **forklift** can handle up to 10 tons!

Loggers use the rugged **skidder** to haul huge logs down the side of the mountain. Some skidders can carry up to three tons of logs at a time in their powerful claws!

The **rocket** blasts into outer space to carry equipment, like satellites, into orbit.

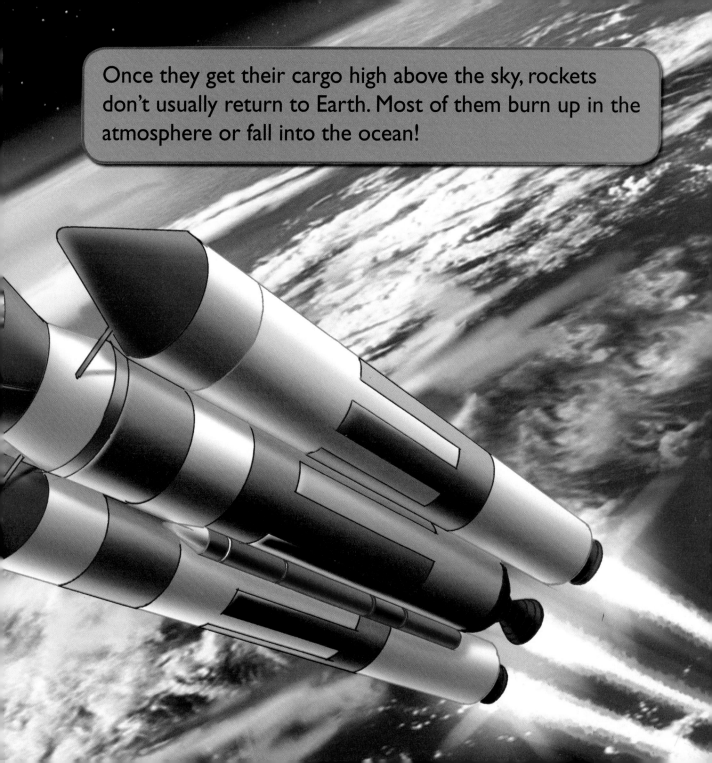

Once they get their cargo high above the sky, rockets don't usually return to Earth. Most of them burn up in the atmosphere or fall into the ocean!